Little

Kaupio Kohola

By:
Tutu Mele

Little Kaupio Kohola

(cow pee' o   ko ho' la ... meaning Humpback Whale)

By

Tutu Mele

*

Dedication

I would like to dedicate this book to the Kuapio Kohola or humpback whales that migrate from Alaska to the Hawaiian Islands each year. These great whales have been protected since 1966 and return to the warm shallow waters of Hawaii to give birth and breed. They travel over 3,000 miles from the Gulf of Alaska to Hawaii in less than 2 months. They stay from December to May while their babies grow strong for the migration back to Alaska.

They then migrate back to Alaska in May to eat and put on weight in preparation for their migration back to the warm shallow waters of Hawaii. This is a yearly ritual. Humpback calves are considered "kamaaina" or native born Hawaiians since they are born in Hawaiian waters!

This book describes their migration in an easy to read poem that teaches youngsters about the wonderful humpback whales that migrate up and down the seas between Alaska and Hawaii.

*www.hawaiimagazine.com

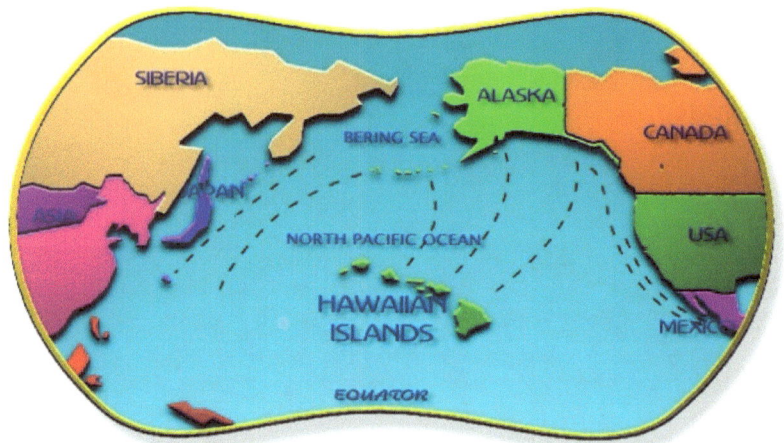

North Pacific Humpback Whale Migration Routes *

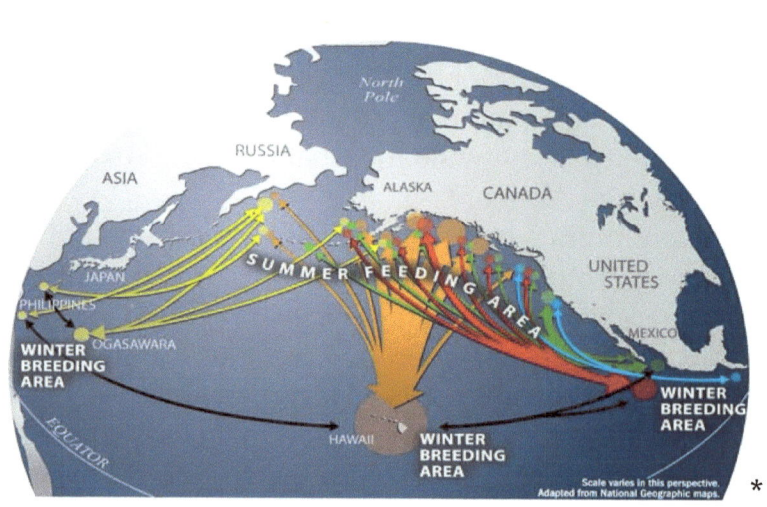

*

Little

Kaupio Kohola

By:
Tutu Mele

Little Kuapio Kohola
Where were you born?
Down in Kaanapali
Where the water is so warm.

Little Kaupio Kohola
Where will you go?
Up North to Alaska
Where the cold winds blow!

Little Kuapio Kohola
On what will you feed?
I will get fat
On krill, herring and squid!

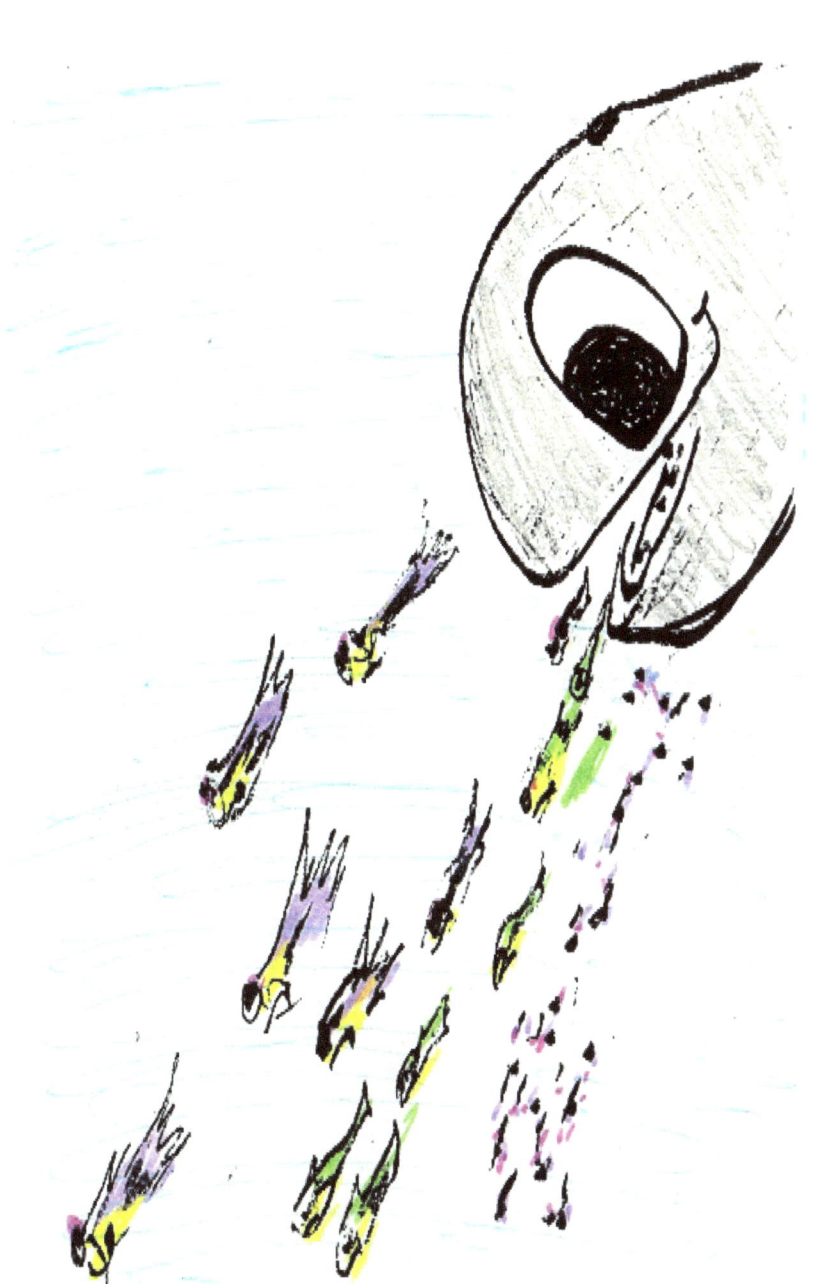

Little Kuapio Kohola
With whom will you play?
With seals and eskimos
And the big manta ray!

Now that you are as big as can be.
Do you have the urge
To swim south to Maui and the
warm sea?

There you will have
A calf of your own
And you can teach her
The oceans to roam.

There is so much to see
And so much to do.
We want to protect
The creatures like you!!!

We will keep you safe
As you travel on your way
So we can see you
Another Spring Day!!!

When I take my children
Down to the sea,
They will see you
And you will see me!

Tutu Mele

  This book is dedicated to my grandchildren who are learning to read and love the excitement of the outdoors. They love looking for the spouts and sprays of the humpback whales as they go on their yearly migration from the Hawaiian Islands to Alaska.

  This yearly migration is in poetry format which is fun for youngsters to read. I hope you and your child enjoy learning about the humpback whales of Hawaii. Whether your child can read or enjoys being read to, he or she will enjoy this book.

  This book is part of a nature series to teach young children about the wonders of nature around them. Other books in this nature series are "Changing Colors", The Frog That Croaked" and "The Ugly Bug".

  Tutu Mele wrote these books over 25 years ago and with the help of her friend and fellow author, Rhonda Feltman, she has finally found a way to publish and share them with beginning readers. She lives in the White Mountains of Arizona and on the Sea of Cortez in Baja California and is constantly inspired by nature.

Little Kuapio Kohola
Vocabulary

Little	Kuapio	Kohola	where
feed	you	born	down
in	the	south	water
is	so	warm	go
up	north	to	cold
winds	blow	on	were
get	fat	krill	herring
squid	whom	play	seals
eskimos	be	urge	swim
sea	calf	your	own
teach	her	ocean	roam
there	much	protect	keep
creatures	like	slow	day
safe	travel	another	spring
manta	ray	children	see
crossing	Hawaii	Maui	Alaska

This book is part of a nature series.
Other titles by Tutu Mele include:

The Ugly Bug

The Frog That Croaked

Changing Colors

Little Whale Small

The Bike That Ate Dirt

Little Dog Laugh